The Tree Poets

The Tree Poets

Shades of Fire

Jane Burn

Jane Lovell

Frank McHugh

First published 2025 by The Hedgehog Poetry Press

Published in the UK by
The Hedgehog Poetry Press
5, Coppack House
Churchill Avenue
Clevedon
BS21 6QW

www.hedgehogpress.co.uk

ISBN: 978-1-913499-86-0

Copyright © Mark Davidson 2025

The right of Mark Davidson to be identified as the editor of this work has been asserted in accordance with the Copyright, Designs and Patents Act 1988. All rights for individual works retained by the respective author.

All rights reserved. No part of this publication may be reproduced, stored in or introduced into a retrieval system, or transmitted in any form, or by any means (electronic, mechanical, photocopying, recording or otherwise) without prior written permissions of the publisher. Any person who does any unauthorised act in relation to this publication may be liable for criminal prosecution and civil claims for damages,

9 8 7 6 5 4 3 2 1

A CIP Catalogue record for this book is available from the British Library.

Jane Burn 7

    River of Broken Things 9
    The Endless Wellbeing of Water 10
    How the Sun Brings Out 11
    Harvest time. The Weather Breaks 12
    Blood on the Snow 13

Jane Lovell 15

    In Tollund Fen 16
    Beautiful Georgiana in death pose at the Royal Tyrrell 18
    Arthur Biley Esq., ... 20
    The Pequegnat Clock 22
    The Hollowing 24

Frank McHugh 25

    surface tension 26
    timeslip 28
    the death of picasso 29
    the cut 30
    morrowing 31

JANE BURN

RIVER OF BROKEN THINGS

The flood took everything. A whole caravan,
its static rooms lifted from bricked roots – little plastic
skylights, slim-fit doors, chassis flung to the swim.

The river was relentless, swashed with run-off mud.
Sent its ridded flot, its gathered muddle of life, its mix-up
down, fast. Gouging scoops of bank, snapping trees

as if they were stair rods, there was nothing, nothing
could stop it. Days and days and days. It took one layer
of homes away, drowned the next two – they emptied slowly,

draining over the years. Some folk rebuilt, some never returned –
their cabins wearing desolate skins of muck, gardens given
to Balsam's purple grip. A digger flattened the ground, cleared

the crush of rubble after people had scrounged what they could
from the mud – silted pans, dented stoves, ruined keepsakes,
precious things. Turf has grown above the scarred land,

where a sense of pity seems to hang. A sense of frailty,
of time biding. A shipping container sticks on a bend, crumpled.
We marvel at the blue paint, rusted – the way its stomach groans

with the water's move. Rich or poor, young or old, stone or wood
it took the lot, left strange reminders – a chimney, with no walls
around it. The skeleton of a mallard, spread along an avenue of shrubs.

A shire horse in the shallows, made from pot – one ear, two legs
missing, harness ripped from its back. Half a cup – *Souvenir*
of where, forever un-said. A caddy for TEA, without a lid.

THE ENDLESS WELLBEING OF WATER

The warm spring sun writes the underfoot cobbles
with sunken light. My wading gently parts the skin
of drowned blossom – my boots move slowly through
the floating lace that they have laid. Young brown trout,

quick as sparks needle the riverbed shallows, while
the older fish scythe the air with silver to catch the flies.
One of a pair of swans skiffs my way and I think
how folk say *they can break a man's arm*, but he

is barely curious, does not hiss. I breathe in the calm
as trains segue past on the opposite bank. The passengers
have this tempting view of the river's rambling flow –
their heads fill the windows as if each carriage

was a canteen of orderly spoons. With each engine's pass,
I wave. Sometimes, one will reflect my wish and wave back.
Some look down at me, askance. Some of them smile –
kindreds, ready join me, splash their way in. Become

the size of a dot, become washed by the current's power,
be rinsed afresh. Sometimes it's good to be flotsam.
Be released by the water – standing, feet bubbled,
legs cooled, faces tilted towards the day, heads hot.

HOW THE SUN BRINGS OUT

A streak of hot elevenses bright has beckoned
next door's Steve from his sanctum, seeded his mind
with barbecue aspirations. His clipped, thinning
fuzz remains in denial beneath the crumpled cloche

of a battered fisherman's hat as he toasts the Gods
that brung this clement, birdy day with his bubbling cup,
crinkles and nods, slurps and sighs, squats at the knee.
I ought to pipe up, let my presence be known

but I am enjoying my bit of being a nosey parker,
sticky-beak watching the bliss of his squint-eyed worship.
Back off the rigs, he has spent the last two weeks at sea –
I love his revel in solid earth, this green-plugged finding

of land legs again. I know he hates to go but needs must
and bills don't pay themselves. These moments
of knowing peace, of planted self, of seeing happiness
from nothing but someone's face in the sun, of seeing

a smile open like petals from a sweet pea's wrinkled bud
are treasures. To make him look, I drop my broom –
over the honeysuckled fence comes half his head
in radiance, half his head in gloom. He has plants

to offer, ready for re-potting. Cucumber – soon
the swelling of gourds, swung from finger-thick stems,
bottle green, bumped with papules that catch the light.
Tomatoes – summer will boil them bloodshot.

Steve is going to mow and crop, pluck and clip –
everything will grind its wheels of growth, search
for synthesis with the sky. To know such dazzle
is to have already stood in shade – to recognise

the value of both. The length of day is marked
by the travel of shadows. I am waiting for glory
to be shawled by dimmet's soft grey cast –
for brilliance to become the quieted wonder of dusk.

HARVEST TIME. THE WEATHER BREAKS

The fields are scalped – a couple of hours
with big machines and the tide of wheat
is drained. Whiskers of stubble crack
under our feet. Before the combine's
rolling blades, we mourn for the flight
of wild creatures – their bee-lulled home
has turned against them, fooled them
with false safety, swelled them with a bounty
of summer's glut. The waiting men un-crack
their arm-slung guns and shoot at the pheasants,
mice and rabbits as they run. A dog-sized hare
defies the acres. Bullets do not match its speed.
Corn-shred spikes the heavy, sullen air – dust
settles on our skin, our hair, the just-swept path.
Straw is sucked and spat out in bound geometry
from the baler's guts. The noise is rhythmic,
the *hum-humming* of its efficiency almost done.
Far around, the land is stripped – dusk wears
a troubled sky. All night the anger of the Earth
is brought in welts of lightning, fears of thunder,
rolling giants of wet-fat cloud. The morning brings
a landscape of waste, a tyre-gouged trample,
a silent damp. Every few yards, the sodden hulk
of a big yellow square, left out in last night's rain.

BLOOD ON THE SNOW

Fresh,   stained.   Blood
                          from innocent things,
a pity wash of scarlet, payment
                       in wound-red coins,
a spangle of thick-clotted gore. There has been
                       much killing here.

Blood, mottling the spoor, pricked
through the thin skim of frozen crust –
the dibble-dabble one leg, two leg, back legs, hop.
The lightfoot passage of sweet-bob,
fluff-baby wickle babbits. There must have been
                dozens of them. Armies of them,
paths criss-crossing, every so often   stop,   scratch
through to the earth for the sweet-hidden stalks
of survival grass. Brown bobbles of excrement,
stain spoiling around them.

There are no notched bones,
              no gnawed skulls,
                 no rended limbs,
               no paws.
There are no other signs of the dead.

JANE LOVELL

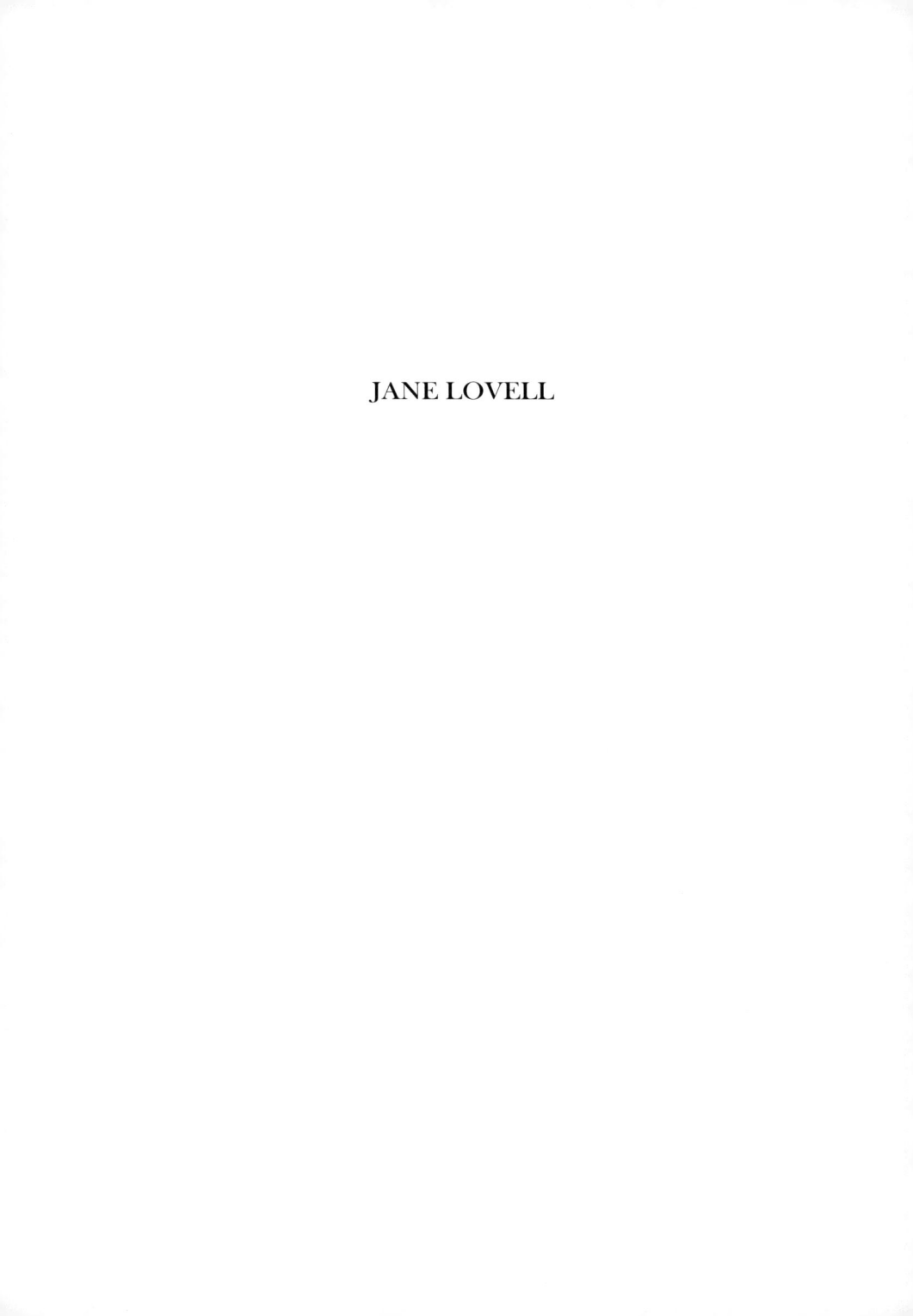

IN TOLLUND FEN

It held him, this desolate land, deep in the soil's dark rinse, its felted mash of moss and fern; kept tight his knuckled spine, steeped skin, the finely-plaited noose.

We find him,
twenty centuries pressed like a leaf
in the wet peat, its acid brew;
his perfect face as if in sleep,
as if in prayer.
We touch his cheek,
our own fragile skin so pale.

We peel back the soil. His thigh sliced by the spade juts bone.

His last moments, bound
and stunned, he summoned
the moon and the dancing girl,
dreamt her trampling
the small figure of a horse,
lost her to a swarm of silent bees,
the rattle of aspen against crow.

Around his throat, the plaited hide.
His spine we find intact, no ruck of vertebrae: the slow stricture of a short drop.

Cloudshift and his skin is lit,
his furrowed brow, the glint
of stubble on his lip.
There is the blue air, the sun lying
long across the marsh,
a lark rising.

There is the serenity of him:
separated from us by sleep.

The secrets he kept, whispers of the ploughed land - barley,
knotweed, camomile and flax - we decipher, find tales of hunger, find
winter in his final breath.

Horsedrawn to Engesvang,
they take him, packed in soil,
past the old Bølling Lake
shivering with sky.

Against the grating of the wheels,
we listen to the wind in the aspen,
a lone snipe jarring the sweep
of the fen.

BEAUTIFUL GEORGIANA IN DEATH POSE AT THE ROYAL TYRRELL

I find you at the end of the hall
prone and twisted. Your exquisite skin,

each taut muscle, your upturned throat,
betray the last throes of existence.

People murmur at your terrible beauty,
the impossible curve of your spine.

Fixed by rays of unforgiving light
you wait to be released,

your prince clattering through some grey dawn
to arrive at the tower of stone.

I wait for darkness, silence held at bay
by my own breathing,

ease open the perspex casing, touch you.
Your mouth is open.

I feed you small mammals, insects, worms,
place them on your tongue, revive you.

Flesh creeps and fattens on your bones;
your eyes charge with lizardy light.

You stretch each pitted limb and snap
your jaws, struggle to your feet, sway

left and right, seeking. You are formidable;
I am suddenly conscious of my own soft flesh.

We leave by the back stairs, avoiding
the laser sensors, the security guard.

You follow me home keeping to the shadows,
dipping and hissing at passing dogs,

gaunt and awkward in your dated leather,
black tongue flickering in the curious air.

ARTHUR BILEY ESQ.,

grocer, tea-taster, amateur magician

he ducked down below the skyline,
set out his table,
its green felt bright as moss,
cups, coins, dice,

the rabbit that popped out of the hat
(it wasn't real of course,
did not flinch at the impact of shells
shaking the very bones of the world,
clods of earth raining down
on its nylon fur);

the wand was purely for effect,
a snapstring telescopic toy,
it could not halt the zip zip
of bullets pinging past him
ploughing into soil, spiriting
those puffs of dust skywards

and sweet Diane, who lay scrunched
to be sawn in two,
had those precious legs blown off,
and the threads, the jelly of them,
all bloodwet like that,
he said
you shouldn't be here
you shouldn't

he watched her trickle away
into the ground, leafmash
in the creases of her neck, her hair,
and everything went quiet then
because he couldn't bring her back
he couldn't say his bloody
abracadabras and make it all vanish
in the swish of a black hat

and after he was discharged
like a small white lamp winking
in a dark night,
back in his grocer's shop
he stacked everything in pyramids,
fanned the paper bags with a flourish,
tasted in the tea
black soil, blood, the metallic
tang of loss

THE PEQUEGNAT CLOCK

Within three weeks, his life was dismantled,
driven north in lofty green vans to be auctioned:
carpets, photographs and clocks,
clocks on every wall and surface,
the whole proceedings measured in clicks
and tocks.

We take him home, smiling in a cutting
of his Compton on the Queen Elizabeth,
his fingers still wavering across the quilt.

With the ticking of the Pequegnat, he drifts in,
takes his place at the keys,
hair swept sideways and eyes on the bottle,
eyes the hue of the sea
if it held its colour in your palm.

Others are here: the donkey man
and Ivy from the Golden Hind, Miss Lovely 1957,
Mr B. the Bikeman, hands coked up from fixing
chains and spokes.

We settle on the sofa, on the edge of the bed.
Mr. John Russell Esq. pulls out the stops,
and we're away on the rollercoaster
of the tutti frutti Melotone:

ice-cream swirls of polka-skirted girls
tripping on their red heels from Rossi's to the pier,
their teasing, and the sweetness of vanilla
studded with bright fruits – stumps of angelica,
glacé cherries you could shine a light through;

voices undulating on the air from the beach
and boating lake;
love drawn in the damp sand with a stick
punctuated by remnants of tiny, crushed crabs.

And while the clock keeps ticking he plays on:
"Waltzing in the clouds", "Serenata",
a smile on his lips, the tang of vinegar cockles
on his breath,
and those long hot days spread out before him
in a shimmer of lipstick and sugar.

THE HOLLOWING

He grows translucent. Beyond him, through him,
the garden wavers as if underwater. A geranium

on the sill fills his ribcage like a blown heart,
its leaves green lungs scalloped like gills, stalks

a map of atoms. He gives off a strange light, muted,
woven. Something chemical: yellow gauze peeled

from soft paraffin, an old bruise turning.
She moves closer, looks through him, sees

an altered world, strange distortions of line and angle.
He stills her with his eyes, reaches out and grasps

her arm. Watery fingers dissolve like tears
in the wool; words erupt as if released from dream.

She hears his goodbyes, catches sky in that last
long look: clouds, a rogue moon, and then he is gone:

blood, lymph, gnarled lungs, all lost in shadow.
It took three months to possess him, a relentless

invasion moving determinedly along the grain,
the ticking of tiny jaws champing, re-shaping, creating

this curved, hollow structure. She lays him out,
his bones brittle with it, honeycombed,

held only by air.

FRANK MCHUGH

SURFACE TENSION

when the fascists pour their fetid water
from golden pails
into free running rivers
when the tears of separated children drip
down through many many layers of bedrock
onto the pillows of my sleeping children
when red crosses run and seep
real blood
will I be sponge or stone?

the sponge that absorbs, soaks up
carries the weight and stench away,
wringing one of them out
somewhere parched and cracked
or full of ferns and undergrowth-
where would there be less damage?
the taking sponge, the martyr sponge
heavy with burden, more liquid than sponge

    or the stone, turning my back, letting it all run off
    using my camber to keep dry,
    calling on my volcanic bonding
    summoning my fiery, pressured lineage
    refusing to let anything enter or change me
    save a temporary surface slickness
    which is forgiveable

You can clean and comfort with a sponge, he says
    You can fight and build with a stone, she says

You can carry the sponge with you always, he says
    The stone will still be there when you get back she says

You can wet your lips with the sponge, he says
    Not 'til you raise the water level with the stone, she says

so I wrapped the stone in sponge
and have both in my hand, right now
I could show you either or both
or I may not show my hand at all
but that depends or whether you carry
love or hate in yours.
                        Show me your hand

First published in Gutter

TIMESLIP

When I drag my sorry ass upstairs at night
the light from my phone shines through
the water in my glass on to my stairwell.
It casts a crystalline reflection

that to those poor souls still living here in the past
is a slow-moving apparition, inexplicable
unsteady and out of time.
I am haunting my own house.

I can hear their confusion as they watch it
feel their fear and fascination
but the old woman doesn't mind, calls it her 'Gloriana'
and blesses herself when I pass.

Her mother was a traveller from Galway
so I'm just another anomaly
when you've been raised on a diet of bloody men
nailed to trees, their hearts outside their chests.

There's a boy who stays weekends with his uncle
in the upstairs room. He cries if he sees the reflection.
I switch the light off but the dark makes my face visible to him
so I've taken to humming a lullaby, like that would help.

I spotted the boy's pinched face in a brown photograph
in the village museum. He looked gaunt, ill
as he stared at the lens, out the photograph
trying to communicate with his eyes, with me.

THE DEATH OF PICASSO

Two bullocks in the gloaming stag-shunting,
                Picasso awoke as the sun was fading
cube heads joined, hazy in the snort clouds,
                half his room facing him, half in profile.
equal engines, opposite and stone thud heavy.
                Every truth he knew, the simple and the twisted,
The lazier grazers move aside,
                sparked around his fingertips.
the fading clouds part to give
                A purplish breeze, lemon and herb-laden
the Greeks above, who love a bull,
                filled and floated a north african curtain
a better view.
                which showed him a gilded sky,
Marcel Marceau in the guise of a heron,
                a disarming, pitying, godless sky.
is disturbed by these peasants
                The weight of it hurt his head
for absolutely the last time
                made his shaved head sore,
and takes off in monochrome
                sore with possibilities and fading things.
with the same noise my father makes
                He felt all of himself disintegrate,
getting out of his armchair, preceded by
                the atoms rearranging as something else,
an accented and audible 'p'tain'
                changed, no longer Pablo,
dropping from his deliberate gallic wingflap.
                like a chorizo is no longer a pig.

        Like a still smouldering Gauloise
that last line lands with a fizz in the mud beside me.
                'like a chorizo is no longer a pig.'
Dusk falls.   Blankets them all.
Peace.

THE CUT

A shimmering bird hangs

                    above a cut of land
which slopes away vertiginously
to the grey watching sea. Patiently inhaling,
exhaling, dry salt, sand

                    and moon drawn shells.
Cast in light, the bird is a helium Christ
suspended in jellied air: laws of atom,
of the physical, of fishing

                  don't apply, or are bow-bent
by sunlight skating through wind,
and a dearth of earthly gravity.

MORROWING

Life here is full of tomorrows,
there was one here   yesterday
and another one   will be round tomorrow
tomorrow's   tomorrow
and the day after

                    Tomorrow and tomorrow.
To morrow *(v):*
to wallow self indulgently in a melancholy state
as a direct result of not living in the present.
As in,
"He morrowed around the house in aimless sloth."

Tomorrow, you're always a day way.
Yesterday all my troubles seemed so far away.
Yestre'en the queen had four Marys,
the nicht she'll hae but three.
Will you still love me tomorrow?
Tomorrow and tomorrow and tomorrow.

  tomorrow is the rhizome of all misery
  tomorrow is the day our ship comes in
  tomorrow will hold you in the curve of its hand
  tomorrow will be as black as the earl of hell's waistcoat
  tomorrow will begin with sucking doves
  tomorrow will end with your lover's perfect back
  tomorrow will be another country
  tomorrow has no map, no language
  is where that girl lives, who keeps on not waking up
  tomorrow the inspector might call
  tomorrow there may be benediction
  tomorrow your daughter will return with your heart in her hand
  tomorrow your son will leave with it
  tomorrow you will walk free
  tomorrow you will feel the sun on your face in the stillness of a long evening
  tomorrow there will be blossom and waxwings
  tomorrow you will feel no need
                        to morrow.